At the Edge of Mercy

Poems by

Kendall Bradley

Copyright © 2020 by Kendall Bradley

All rights reserved.

ISBN 978-1-62806-275-5 (print | paperback)

Library of Congress Control Number 2020907310

Published by Salt Water Media
29 Broad Street, Suite 104
Berlin, MD 21811
www.saltwatermedia.com

Cover image and author photo courtesy of the author

*What would people look like
if we could see them as they are,
soaked in honey, stung and swollen,
reckless, pinned against time?*

- Ellen Bass

Table of Contents

The Gathering 1

Roar 2

Scars 3

A Poem Might 4

Beginning 5

Return 6

Mortality 7

On the Deck 8

Falling in Love with the Mind of Eudora Welty 10

Seaside 11

The Burn 12

The Dig 13

We Make Trite the Beauty of the Rose 14

Crepuscular 15

Science Class Daydream 16

On Making the Most of Each Moment 18

Gnomes 20

Chance Encounter 21

Want in the First World 22

And So It Goes 23

A Moment of Insight and Clarity	25
This Life	26
Sometimes Poetry Is Like Guerilla Warfare	27
Daybreak after a Night of Angry Drinking	28
Railroad Towns	29
At the Edge of Mercy	30
Moonrise over Parramore Island	31
Adverbial Blessing	32
Unspoken	33
13 Ways of Looking at Razor Wire	34
Kaufman	36
The Trap	37
Spinoza's God	38
Conversation with Myself under a Full Moon	39
Another Poem for Robert	41
The Last War	43
Question	44
Man Walking in the Rain, Unrequited	45
Inexorable	46
Box Tree Road Tryst	47
Every Rock and Every Stone	48
The Beautiful	49

Retrospect 50

Abandoned House in Moonlight 51

Speaking of Sorrow 52

Voices 53

Bicycle Chronicles 54

Believe in This 56

Waiting Room Blues 57

Who Will Stand? 60

So and Not So 62

Still Life with Apple 63

When Truth Is No Longer Truth and Lies Are No Longer Lies .. 65

As If Beneath a Bodhi Tree 66

Two Ruminations on Growing Old 67

Change 70

Death of a Poem 71

Darkness 72

One Autumn Evening 73

If I Am Honest with Myself 74

Streets of the Night 75

Dung Beetles and Eye Winkers 76

Thinking Back 60 Years, Remembering Sam 77

Looking 79

Jump 80

On the Porch 81

Truth Be Told 82

Rancor 83

My New Book 84

Soldiers of Fortune 85

My Days 86

Late March 2020 87

When All Has Been Taken from Me 89

The Gathering

Tonight,
as I lie awake,
a host of poems
rides west upon
the sea wind.

I can hear them
in the trees
as the branches
scrape against
the side
of the house.

In no time at all
they are in,
rustling inside
the walls
as they move down
from the attic.

When I turn on
the bedroom light,
I see them scurrying
across the floor,
these creatures
from another
world.

Roar

A sojourner
moving along the arc of time,
destination unknown,

is caught
in the net of meaning

becomes an inmate in the prison
of language

struggles to break free

becomes a cloud, a bird,
a speck of dust

becomes a roaring wind
on an empty plain.

Scars

As for scars,
I'll take
the visible ones
every time.
At least they
are out in
the open
and we
usually know
how we got
them.
It's the
invisible ones,
lurking in
our own inner
darkness,
that give us
the most
trouble.
We tend
to forget
all about them
until they begin
to fester
without
warning.

A Poem Might

Smolder
in your hand

turn fireflies
into music

lick you
from the inside

exfoliate
your dreams

make
a silent scream

conjure
a wanton smile

from the moon.

Beginning

I was adrift on a vast
and uncharted inner sea,
an unwilling mariner
becalmed beneath
blazing stars fixed
like fierce eyes upon
a rigid sky.

And I was dying
of thirst.

Then I heard you,
faintly at first,
like a soft wind,
calling my name
from a distant shore
of the outer world

and I felt myself moving,
moving slowly but
inexorably over the waves
toward landfall
and the safety of
your voice.

Return

Memory curls
around these old trees
like wood smoke
that has no escape.

On the ground are
deciduous leaves,
deer droppings,
and thick shats
from loblollies
which muffle my steps.

I find the ditch,
now choked
with dead fall,
and the acrid smell
of stagnant water
closes in as I cross

to the small clearing
which was once
the beginning
of a field
that grew strawberries
and asparagus.

Soon, I stumble
on sheets of rusted tin,
remnants from the barn roof,
the rafters long since rotted
into the loam.

This means I am getting
close to where the house
once stood
and I see the spot,

a pile of rubble
obscured by honeysuckle
and closer to the barn
than I remember.

Mortality

The morning is
an albatross
forced from the sea,
bleeding from
its eyes.

Opaque forms
that seem to be people
move at the edge
of things,
beyond purpose
or intent.

A sullen wind arises.

Shadows
of shadows,
convex and concave,
dance in unison,
cry out,

lift their arms
toward me
as winged creatures
fly out of their
stubbed fingers

and stream inside me
to a place
that could be my heart.

They are brazen,
and I am afraid
they will eat me
alive, from
the inside out.

I feel them begin,
first a slight shudder,
then the gnawing
pain.

On the Deck

Finally we are
here together
and it's time
for the annoying
and troublesome
thoughts that are
the detritus of
the day to dissipate,
and they do so
grudgingly among
the cloud swirl
and early stars
of a broad sky.

I contemplate
the dark leaves
of maples
and wild cherry
along the borders
of the yard
and think
perhaps it's a
simple matter
of setting boundaries
at the edge of
the things
that somehow
take us in the wrong
direction.

Not such an easy
task when it
comes down to it.

A human life
is such
a frail thing
and intentions
can be frailer
still.

As you pour me
another glass
of wine,
I watch our cat,
who doesn't need
forgiveness
or redemption,
chase a doomed
insect into the night

and out on
the highway,
truckers run through
their gears,
destinations known
only to themselves.

We share a very
close life, you and I,
and I try to push aside
the nagging thought
that we all must
die alone in the end.

Last night,
I dreamed of
being skinned
alive by a faceless
antagonist,
with you watching,
frozen in horror,
from an upstairs
window of my
childhood home,
destroyed by fire
nearly fifty years
ago.

Falling in Love with the Mind of Eudora Welty

I think of a faded,
dusty road in Mississippi
which leads to the other side
of something that
somehow matters
or somehow doesn't,
where pain is a flower
pressed between memories
of personal disaster or
the failure of progeny.

I think of a landscape
where grotesque shapes
can take form to promote
a fortuitous understanding
that is an accident of being.

I think of a song wherein
lives are drowned
in a river of tribulation
or transformed by
a lightning strike,
where the razor of chance
cuts the tendons and ligaments
which hold time together,
where gods and devils dance
on the rusting rooftops
of shotgun shanties
and in the gardens
of the ignobly dispossessed,

where the lost and the damned
and even the joyful of spirit
are the survivors of a tragedy
none can expunge from
time or memory.

Seaside

1
Here at the edge
of the continent,
at the borderland of
time and tide,
I discover
salt-gnarled cedars
and stunted pines
framing my view
to the east.

I find the mud-flat
hieroglyphics of heron tracks
and clam signs,
witness the ephemeral
dance of wind and light
over the broad bays,
catch the quick shadows
of sand sharks
in the shallows,
hear the osprey's
piercing cry before
its taloned plunge.

2
Beyond the reach
of upland swales
and rusting marine railways,
out past the dark marshes
and oyster cultches,
beyond the shifting barrier islands
the white capped sea awaits.
Its distance-muffled roar
of transcendent indifference
seems to suggest a cadenced
and insistent prophecy
which yet remains
indecipherable and vague,
perhaps too strange
for human ears.

The Burn

The slow burn
of mediocrity,
the quick burn
of genius,

the fire consumes
us all
in the end

even the wise
even the brave
even the masterful
even the gentle
and kind

utterly consumed
by the fire

that is a flower
that is a gun
that is hatred
that is love
that is ignorance
that is bliss
that is a shadow
that is a dream
of water
in a dry,
dry land.

The Dig

How deep
do I need to dig
to perform an
archaeology
of the self?

If I seek out
the psychic artifacts
of my life,
scattered in layers
along the fault lines
and fissures of
the years,

if I scour
the detritus
of my personal
rubble heaps,
looking for clues
of who I am
and what I have
become,

if I carefully
bring up the fragments
one by one
into the light
of day,

how will I know
if I have truly
dug deep enough,

or if the pieces
of the puzzle
I would solve,
like so many
random shards
of flint or pottery,
can ever be
cobbled together
into a meaningful
whole?

We Make Trite
the Beauty of the Rose

We make trite
the beauty of the rose

yet are quick to rend
our flesh on the thorns
of life.

For the taste of blood
we suffer the primacy
of pain

and let the beauty
slip away

to a place just
beyond our reach

where it shimmers
like a dare.

Crepuscular

They are not
from another
world but
from this one.

Neither animate
nor inanimate,
they slip
effortlessly
through the crack
between real
and unreal
that opens
briefly in
the dim light.

Their mission
is obscure.

Perhaps they come
to rearrange
the molecular
structure of frogs,
mix infinity
and rain water,
steal the souls
of babies,
turn words
into leaves,
or thoughts into
droning insects.

They leave
as suddenly
as they come
and no one
is the wiser
as night moves
in.

Science Class Daydream

In the midst of
of a tedious lecture,
an errant word
fell by chance upon
the dissection table,
squirming briefly
then lying still,
splayed in silence
upon the cold
stainless steel.

Just what word
met such a demise
was impossible
to tell but
it became at once
an object of curious
investigation
as it seemed to be
neither animal,
nor vegetable,
nor mineral
but a different
life form altogether.

Upon inspection,
its outer membrane
appeared soft
but difficult to pierce.

Once breached
by the scalpel,
the integument
gave way and
forceps laid bare
an inner geography
of strangeness,

a self-contained
cosmos of primordial
and intricate pathways,
an organic circuit board

leading to numberless
clusters of smoldering
fire

which quickly
burned out
and vanished
beneath the
unforgiving glare
of an incandescent
bulb.

On Making the Most of Each Moment

If we could do this,
if we could do this
with absolute consistency
how different the world
would be.

It would be magical.

Love and happiness
would have a chance.
Smiles would openly gather
in public places.
Poetry would thrive.
Artists would proliferate.
Spontaneous singing
and dancing would
become commonplace.

And yet, if we did this,
the status quo
would be annihilated.
The trains and planes
wouldn't run on time.
Pharmaceuticals would tank.
The entire economy
would take a hit.
Politicians and preachers
would lose their con
and public opinion
would begin to turn.

At the urging of
the military-industrial complex,
those making the most
of every moment
would be condemned
as enemies of the people,
gathered up and imprisoned
by the authorities.

In dimly lit
piss-stained chambers

heavy handed goons
would torture
the magic out of them
and then return them
to the outer world,
disoriented,
cringing in the light,
no longer able
to make the most
of anything.

Gnomes

Their smiles
were paradoxical
but their laughter
seemed cruel
as they stood
unperturbed,
the house
burning down
behind them.

Chance Encounter

It was late
one night
at a time
when shadows
take on a luminous
quality and
memories tend
to snag in
the present
for no apparent
reason
that I encountered
a former self
who had been
absent for
many years.

After initial
salutations and
a brief catching up
over necessary
libations,
it became
apparent that
we really did not have
much in common.

I found him
strange and intense
and he judged me
to be such
a disappointment
he would not
allow me to pass
the muster of
his own easy
arrogance.

So we parted
company without
ceremony and went
our separate ways
without a backward
glance and with no
lingering regrets.

Want in the First World

Let's face it,
we are wired to want
so quite naturally
that is what we do
and we have made
an art form of it.
It is good for
the economy
and the brokers
of power,
this ceaseless
wanting.
It is good for
televangelists and
drug dealers.
Moving beyond
the basic necessities
to face lifts
and tummy tucks,
we are so good
at wanting, so bad
at letting go.

And So It Goes

A scornful Socrates
choosing hemlock
over exile.

Diogenes living in a pot,
asking Alexander the Great
to get out of his light.

Seneca opening his veins
at the order of Nero.

Hypatia stripped, mutilated
and burned by a Christian mob.

Abelard
becoming a eunuch
for the sake of love.

Giordano Bruno
by papal decree
burned alive at the stake,
his tongue tied
with a rope.

Spinoza persecuted by Jews
and Christians alike
for his concept of God.

Voltaire and Rousseau
locked in a grudge match.

Kant with his OCD.

Kierkegaard giving up
and taking his leap
of faith.

Nietzsche taking Europe by storm
before becoming clinically insane
and dying of syphilis.

Wittgenstein declaring
he had solved all
the problems of philosophy
then becoming the loudest critic
of his own magnum opus.

Heidegger and Hitler
and *Gleichschaltung*.

Camus and Sartre
friends then enemies
to the death
over the question of
revolutionary violence.

Gödel with his iophobia,
dying of malnutrition.

And so it goes.

A Moment of Insight and Clarity

When he was
12 years old,
standing on a bridge
spanning a small
salt water gut
filled with minnows
at low tide,
he accidently blew off
part of his thumb
and index finger
with a silver salute.
No shock stunned
minnows floated
white bellied to
the surface that day
and it was a long
walk back home,
with the pain
throbbing like a
fish quivering
in the bottom
of a scow.

This Life

How long does it take
our faces to be absorbed
by the hardened masks
we wear over
and over again
in performance
of the desperate rituals
of daily life?

How many hard
and soft miles
have we traveled
to be exactly where we are
right now?

All we have,
all we have ever had
are the days and nights,
the diurnal rhythm
of our expectations.

All we have,
all we have ever had
are the ceaseless intersections
of time and place
cast and recast
upon the indifferent
grid of fate,
sometimes to our liking
and sometimes not.

We watch a pantomime
of leaves in the wind,
trying to cipher a little
sense out of it all,
our sorrows etched in
the mundane face of time,

our hopes still blazing
like hot stars on the tightly
shut eyelids of eternity.

Sometimes Poetry Is Like Guerilla Warfare

The poems have had enough
and have banded together
to take over the high ground
of the mind and spirit.
They are in the mountains
where they are drinking wine
beneath a waxing moon
and plotting the coming revolution.

They will descend to the valley,
these fearless poems,
and strategically attack out of nowhere,
inflict casualties on the status quo
and disappear into the splintered air.

The regime, of course, will spare
no expense to find them.
El Presidente will announce
that they shall be hunted down
like wild dogs and butchered,
that their headless torsos
will be drug through the streets
of the capital.

The poems are not worried.
They will die for the cause
if need be.
In the darkness, they will
surreptitiously bring
mangoes and rambutans
and dreams of resistance
to the children of the villages.
Though they will be hunted
with monstrous zeal,
they will take the time
to hang magical lanterns
in the squares of the capital.

Daybreak After a Night of Angry Drinking

Break the bottle
and shred the wind,

gut the night
and watch it bleed.

The sky weeps
for mercy's lack

shedding its stars
one by one.

Railroad Towns

They sprang up
out of farmland
and woods when
the NY, P, & N
laid down the Virginia
track in 1884,
a straight bright
meridian of steel
from New Church
to Cape Charles
which created overnight
prosperity and
sudden wanderlust.

Ghosts of former
travelers to Wilmington
and Philadelphia crowded
the last passenger train
in 1958 on its short run
north to the Maryland line
but the romance
had long since died,
an accidental victim of
unrelenting progress.

Today the rusting rails
have been abandoned
even by the freight lines
and the old station depots
have disappeared or been
turned into storage sheds
or tiny museums.

The towns still stand
but most are smaller
and quieter now,
hunched along
the useless track
like aging jilted lovers
left unceremoniously
on the platforms,
watching their dreams
fade into the distance,
hoping for better days
that will never come.

At the Edge of Mercy

> *What is our innocence,*
> *what is our guilt? All are*
> *naked, none are safe.*   - Marianne Moore

Somewhere near the edge of mercy
many of us die our thousand deaths:
charred beyond recognition
by fires we do not understand,
encapsulated in ice
like mammoths from the Pleistocene,
suffocated in concrete
or lost at sea,
electrocuted by love's frayed wires
or starved to bones by love's lack.

Eventually, we become
prisoners taken in a war of attrition.
Our offenses are many,
too numerous to record,
the hidden voices tell us.
The deaths mount up
inside the walls we have built
for our own penance.

The bells toll around the clock
and the mute guards watch
with familiar faces
from the top of the towers.
Beneath an empty sky
we ask: is there no mercy?

Yet the mercy we seek
is our own to give,
or perhaps our own to allow.

These deaths, these walls
are but illusions we create
from guilty remnants of ourselves
and thus ourselves betray.
Can we not find the courage
to topple the walls,
beat the stones to dust,
and let the prison break begin?

Moonrise Over Parramore Island

The mangled moon
rises from the sea,
a bloody wreck filled
with departed souls.
As they slowly drop
from the astral hull,
they leave a luminous
trail of woe across
the complacent sky.

Adverbial Blessing

- for Phil

May your *whens*
be a miracle of fate,
may your arrivals
and departures be
neither early nor late.

May your *wheres*
find the serendipitous
curve of space
which can lead you,
in time of need,
to a magical place.

May your *hows*
be a paradigm
of simplicity and style
and may you never
have to sport
a disingenuous smile.

May your *whys*
be not tyrannical
but sensible and true,
perhaps with some whimsy
and little ado.

Unspoken

The clamorous
world of noise
teaches us this:

to fear our own silence.

⋅

For the sake of paradox,
let the question be put:

Can silence be heard?

⋅

A poet's words
should lead at last
to the eloquence

of the unspoken.

13 Ways of Looking at Razor Wire

- after Wallace Stevens

1.
The truth of razor wire
lies in the mendacity of its users.
But this is not its only truth.

2.
Before the scorched swallow
became fixed and rigid
upon the high tension line,
it was dreaming of razor wire.

3.
At sundown, razor wire
is a thousand points of blood
for every hundred feet
of coiled steel.
The blood pools briefly
before it disappears
into the quicksand of night.

4.
As ghosts walk
in the garden of death,
the razor wire pretends
to be asleep.

5.
Air Force One has landed
somewhere near the border
of our paranoia.
When the President speaks
from the tarmac,
his words tear at the air,
sharp as razor wire.
He is wildly applauded.

6.
Is razor wire
a symptom or a result
of nameless fear as old as genes?

7.
Somewhere there are memories
of heavy snow and ashes
and lines of dark shapes
huddled beneath the unforgiving
search light shadows of razor wire.

8.
The factory runs three shifts a day
to meet demand.
In the small lunch room,
workers joke and consult
their smart phones
before returning to the craft
of making razor wire.

9.
There are inmates
in asylums for the criminally insane
who dance upon razor wire
like reckless moonbeams escaping
the pull of gravity.

10.
The west Texas wind
blows over the forgotten bones
of Comanches and rabid coyotes.
It whistles through
the empty eyes of razor wire.

11.
Somewhere in the beating heart
of America, there are those who think
that razor wire can protect us
from ourselves.

12.
At night in Arizona, there are
lost children who dream of leaving their cages
to play soccer and eat ice cream.
In the morning, the razor wire
glimmers in the sun.

13.
How many miles of razor wire
do we each carry within the ambagious
chambers of our secret hearts?

Kaufman

The French called
him the American Rimbaud.
The San Francisco police
called him degenerate,
faggot, pinko, nigger.
They broke his bones
with their night sticks
and threw him
in the slammer
time and time again.

But they couldn't break
his spirit, they couldn't
stop the luminous vision
of his crazy genius
from shining forth,
brighter than all
the neon lights on all
the hope shattered
streets of America.

They couldn't silence
his jazz riff beat poetry,
his mad syncopated
hymns to the moon
and the wild beasts
of the heart and mind.

He silenced himself
for ten years after
the murder of JFK
and finally broke that
silence with a poem about
ships that never sailed.

Now, in the blue ecstasy
of dream blood waters,
his ship still sails on
over the hazy seas
like the sweet
ephemeral notes of
North Beach nights
long ago.

The Trap

Confounded
by fate,
snagged by
the steel jaws
of time,
we can spend
an entire lifetime
trying to figure
out which
of our limbs
we need
to gnaw
off.

Spinoza's God

He was a lens grinder
of high regard and
a man of simple needs.
He understood God
to be everything that
is and everything
that can be.

Because his notion
of deity was not
an insecure,
anthropomorphic,
psychopathic bully
with a worship complex,

he was persecuted
most of his life
by Christian and Jew alike,
even stabbed by a zealot
on the steps of a synagogue.

Spinoza kept
his slashed cloak
as a souvenir
and went on to write
one of the greatest
philosophical treatises
in recorded history.

Spinoza one, zealots zero.

Conversations with Myself Beneath a Full Moon

Voice 1:	I feel unsteady,
	blurred around the edges,
	beyond the hope of
	tangible things.

Voice 2:	The moon perambulated
	around the universe
	and when it came back,
	it was inside out
	and moving backwards.

Voice 1:	I have made many promises
	to myself and others,
	broken most and forgotten
	the rest.

Voice 2:	The moon was smiling
	as it floated down
	to walk in a field of
	fox skulls but the
	nightshades were
	waiting in the ditches.

Voice 1:	Death is my shadow
	and thus I now fear
	high noon and cloudy days.

Voice 2:	The moon is master
	of eternal return
	yet its sorrow can
	be heard as endless
	weeping.

Voice 1:	Pain is like water
	seeking its own level
	without regard
	for recrimination.

Voice 2:	The moon is mad
why else would it sing
of silver rings
and centipedes?

Voice 1:	The sin of madness
is truth. This is why
I seek redemption
in the hope of nothingness.

Voice 2:	The moon whispers
that nothingness
is the mother of truth
but redemption is a lie.

Another Poem For Robert

Your car was in the back yard by the woods
near where your body was found
and the battery was dead.
I figured you needed the light at 2:00 AM
to line up the shotgun's stock
precisely against the fence post.
You didn't want any mistakes.

Your house was in perfect order
emptied of almost everything
and the notes you left for each of us
reflected in their totality
relief and a certain alacrity
for the final acceptance
of what you wanted to do.

You were not sick, you said,
but just tired.
Besides, you were looking forward
to talking hoops with Dean Smith
and being reunited with all your
deceased loved ones and cherished pets.
Our grief would last only for a season,
you wrote.

I submit that you were wrong
on all counts and not least the grief.

I realize this was the logical consequence
of not wanting to wake up anymore
to the unpredictable challenges of life
and the threat of more new days.
What you did was your human right
and I have to respect your strength
of will and scrupulous dedication
to the cause of self-destruction.

Yours was the ultimate selfish act
but, perhaps in some way,
it is also selfish for me
to miss your loving presence

in our lives and think daily
about what could have been.

Perhaps it is selfish to be nearly
sickened by sadness as I watch
your granddaughters from afar,
these few years later,
capering into their lives without
ever knowing you.

If so, it's the kind
of selfishness
I've come to live with,
now that you are gone.

The Last War

After the frenzied
words have shriveled
and died from
lack of meaning,
after the furious
fires have burned
themselves out,
after the hungry plagues
have consumed all
they were designed
to consume,

the rats will grow fat
in the kingdom of rats

and the roaches
will grow fat in
the kingdom of roaches.

The eyes which will
look out from the tall
and silent towers,
which in mockery
may yet stand,
will not be human eyes.

They will not stare
in fear at the panorama
of devastation
for which the old
earth will quietly
rejoice.

Question

Will we make
the androids
with such refined
olfactory receptors
that, in the later days
when they
come for us,
they will be able
to sniff us out
with methodical
and relentless
efficiency

in the caves,
in the bunkers
and all
of our other
hiding places
of last resort?

Man Walking in the Rain, Unrequited

He walked in the rain as if
his beating heart was in
his outstretched hand,

as if he was reluctant to bring
it in closer to the gaping
hole in his chest and yet
was afraid of dropping it,

as if he therefore held it
so tightly with both hands
that the warm blood
oozed between his fingers
and dripped upon the street

and was washed away
by the rain in rivulets
of red which slid into
the storm drain
and eventually flowed
unnoticed into the sea.

Inexorable

It's not like
many of us
didn't see
it coming.

It's not like
many of us
didn't speak
out for all
to hear.

It's just that
it's happening

anyway.

It's just that,
in spite of
everything,

it's happening
now.

Box Tree Road Tryst

Halfway to the creek
off Seaside Road,
black gum and salt pines
crowded the ditch banks
and this is where
we stopped the car.

It was late afternoon
on New Year's Eve
and Samba Pa Ti
was playing on the radio.

Recklessly, we got out
and danced slowly,
desperately,
defiantly,
on the cold tar and chip,
unexpectedly
putting on a show
for a lone waterman
on his way
to the landing.

So bittersweet it was
that we still talk about it

after all these years.

Every Rock and Every Stone

As the search
unfolds,
as the flashlights
move carefully
and relentlessly
over the rugged
terrain beneath
the cliff face,
every rock,
every stone
turned over
reveals something
slithery
and unwholesome,
something deadly
or disgusting,
something
furtive,
some slimy
enemy
of light
lurking
beneath
every rock
and every
stone.

The Beautiful

Do not ask if you are able.
Do not ask if you are worthy.

Simply allow yourself
to see the beautiful
to hear the beautiful
to touch the beautiful
to smell the beautiful
and yes to taste
the beautiful.

Do this
over and over
again.

Be the finder
of the beautiful
be the beholder
of the beautiful
experience its
bounty

before it fades
before it dies
before it rots away
before it turns
into a deformity
before it disappears
in front of your eyes

and you wonder
where it has gone
or if it was ever there
in the first place.

Retrospect

A page unturned
a hand is still

an empty glass
on the window sill

the old clock's ticks
become a roar

streaks of sunlight
stain the door.

Abandoned House in Moonlight

In the ramshackle
rooms of the night,

the moon's bones
lie like broken glass
on warped floors
of aged heart pine.

The moon's face
is pinned upon a wall,
caught in a crooked smile
of cracked plaster.

And the lost children
of the moon are here,
shadows which seem
older than time.

They call out to me.

I listen as they
scuttle along
the baseboard
and vanish through
doorways of dream.

I feel them
beckoning to me

from the other side.

Speaking of Sorrow

We bear what
we cannot speak
and speak what
we cannot bear.

Sometimes,
we must endure
our sorrows
in the severe
silence of the
unspeakable.

Yet sometimes,
we have to speak
before the crushing
weight of heartache
pulls us down,

for without
the grace
of words,
the sorrow would
never let us go.

Voices

Sad it is,
the voices
that cry out
with a clear and
noble intent
yet are
ignored,
or mistaken
for mere
background
noise.

Sadder still,
the voices
that have been
silenced,
made mute
as cannon scrap
by the god
of stolen power.

Saddest of all,
the voices
we will never
hear,
the ones
that try
to speak
but to no avail,
helpless
as stones
beneath
an empty
sky.

Bicycle Chronicles

- for Milford

He was a solitary rider
and a man of few spoken
words.

The winding back roads,
which he knew better
than the veins
on the back of his own
sun-darkened hands,
were his private domain
and he put more miles
on two wheels than
many did on four.

His honesty and integrity
were legendary
and he would offer
his help to anyone
who had a need

but he was most alive
on the open road
when he could feel
the wind in his face
and be comfortable
in his own skin
and think his own
quiet thoughts

of sky and woods
of marsh and sea mist,
of little towns
and corn fields,
of October leaves
and ditch bank lilies.

I think he lived for
the smell of sudden rain
on hot tar and chip
and the friendly waves

from gardeners in
wide-brimmed hats

or from winos on tottering
front porches.

Yet we never talked
much about his rides
and all that he saw
from the seat of his
recumbent bike,

because we never talked much
about anything really.

This is why,
when my brother and I
cleaned out our parents'
house before putting
it up for sale,
I painstakingly searched,
though in vain,
for a fantasy of mine:
a diary, a memoir,
or just a sweat-stained
spiral notebook,

hoping against hope
to find secret
bicycle chronicles

written by my dad.

Believe In This

- after Bob Kaufman

Apple seeds and quasars
the immortality of smiles
serendipity
tomato sandwiches
the ability to get it right
the ability to get it wrong
the power of critical thinking
the indifference of cats
broken hearts
secrets
question marks
the speed of light
the speed of darkness
listening
waiting
giving
the mystery of saxophones
geometry
a garden
voices in the wind
laughter
dust to dust
dancing
the unmistakable face of evil
oranges
caterpillars
the smell of cedar.

Waiting Room Blues

I walk in with my usual
wobbling shuffle
and proceed to
the front desk employing

my usual reluctant smile,
register, and pass
up the hand sanitizer
for the time being.

I then find the most
convenient location
as far away from
everyone as I can get

and begin waiting
in an uncomfortable chair
as two young women
near me discuss

the vicissitudes of
the second trimester
and a middle aged man
with a hacking cough

settles in the seat
next to me even though
there are other vacant
chairs further away.

Finding the wi fi to be
somewhat reluctant,
I curse at myself for
forgetting my book and

begin to stare at the bronze
placard on the wall
which lists the names
of the local institutions

and illustrious
eleemosynary personages

who helped make this
community health center

a reality and in so doing
have contributed
at least indirectly
to my current discomfort.

In an attempt to be
broad minded and,
in fairness to my chair,
I begin wondering

if my old bones can indeed
find comfort anywhere
and perhaps my growing
vexation is not due

to a design flaw or to
Chinese robotic disregard.
I watch with waning restraint
as patients are called

and patients depart and
Mr. Hacking Cough is replaced
by Ms. Runny Nose and it seems
the two pregnant ladies

have given birth to
three screaming toddlers who
show no interest whatsoever
in immediate appeasement.

So it is that the longer
I wait the more I want
to carp and the more
I feel an uncontrollable urge

to find fault with human
existence in the modern age
and all my fellow human
beings within eyesight

most of whom are no doubt
having similar thoughts

in which I also am included
with no lack of restraint.

It is at this point that
three attendants wheel in
a gurney on which
a woman about my age lies

with oxygen tubes
in her nose and an IV
in her wrist and they leave
her there alone to wait

and I hesitate to look
at her at first but when
I do she catches my eye
and meekly smiles

as I smile back and
with no small embarrassment
have to wonder, as my name
is finally called for my simple

six month check-up, what is
wrong with me that I so
blatantly forget my own ample
blessings and wonder also

if an asteroid were to take
out the entire planet
in the next few minutes,
how many millions of us

just before impact would be
complaining about the weather,
or tepid coffee, or the long
wait in a doctor's office.

Who Will Stand?

I watch mutely as
eyes once bright
are burned to crisps
in their dark sockets.

I listen as
tongues once bold
fall silent and
crumble into dust
that drifts
with the wind.

I cry as
once warm hearts
are turned to salt
and beat no more.

Who now will stand
against this raging world?

Who will stare down
the ardent faces
of evil intent?

Who will speak words of truth
to the conspiracies of silence?

Who will dare to love
in the kingdom of
abducted hearts?

Where now
are the heroes
of the lost land:

the unheralded and
unanointed ones,
the bold ones
who will stand up
in the hour of need,

the ones
who will confront
darkness with light,

the ones
who will refuse
to be taken
alive?

So and Not So

Believing it is so
doesn't make it so
and believing
it is not so
doesn't make it
not so,

but who is
the arbiter of so
and not so?

Who can perceive
the *ding an sich*
and report it
stark and true?

The teeming universe
is not a plate of facts
but a skein of probabilities
from which we spin
our stories
like cunning spiders

making up the so
and not so
to suit ourselves

and hoping
it works out.

Still Life With Apple

The gala apple
resting upon
the kitchen table
is mottled red
and yellow and green.
It sits part in shadow
part in light,
basking in its
own private
apple mystery.

It appears motionless
yet moves
as the tilted earth moves
while spinning on its axis
at a thousand miles
per hour.

It appears motionless
yet moves as our
elliptical galaxy moves
toward its rendezvous
with Andromeda
at over a million miles
an hour.

It changes depending
on where I stand
in the room,
or whether I look at it
as Cezzane or O'Keefe
might have looked
or if I imagine I am
a worm slowly
tunneling inside.

It is an apple
because its genes
have made it so
and, like everything else
we know,
is a dance of quarks

and leptons
in mostly empty space,
riddled by neutrinos
we cannot see.

It is an apple
because we
have named it so.
It is skin, flesh and seed,
exuding appleness
upon the kitchen table,
just days from becoming
rotten pulp,

and if I eat it now,
it will be crispy,
juicy and sweet,
a simple pleasure
to which worms
can no doubt relate.

When Truth Is No Longer Truth and Lies Are No Longer Lies

The ideal subject of totalitarian rule is not the convinced Nazi or the dedicated communist, but people for whom the distinction between fact and fiction, true and false, no longer exists. - Hannah Arendt

Steal the fruit from
the tree of fear
and eat the sweet poison.
It is not forbidden
but demanded.

When truth is no longer truth
and lies are no longer lies
our tortured reason
is capable of anything.

Hope dies in the streets
torn from limb to limb,
babies die in the womb
afraid of being born.

Heretics burn at the stakes,
innocents swing from the trees
and supplicants grow restless
in the shadows of monuments.

Our deeds will be numbered
our thoughts will be listed
the truth will be twisted
into ropes that bind.

Here come the faces
with plucked-out eyes.
They carry their darkness
in a blanket of forgetfulness.

Here come the faces
with mouths fused shut.
They embrace their silence
like a jewel of salvation.

Here come the faces
which know not truth or lie
and care not
that birds of prey
darken the sky.

As If Beneath a Bodhi Tree

As if beneath
a Bodhi tree,
I contemplate
my overlords,
the coded messages
that make me tick

the sneaky
Darwinian algorithms
that make me
dissatisfied
whether I smile
or weep.

As if beneath a
Bodhi tree,
I contemplate
the paradox
that is time,
and the riddle
that is space.

I contemplate
my own complicity
in all of it,

hoping to find
the lack of me
in any of it.

Two Ruminations on Growing Old

I.
Life has been
what it has been,
jagged edges and
smooth stones,
a bit of glory and
tribulation to spare,
a facing down
of regrets and
recriminations.

I am fortunate
to have known love
but in the process
have been hurt
and have hurt others,
sometimes with the
best of intentions.

If I had to do it
all over again
with the wisdom
of second sight,
maybe I wouldn't make
the same mistakes
but I doubtless
would make
different ones
every bit as human
and every bit
as consequential.

I am finding out
that growing old
is not about
daring to eat
a peach,
it is about daring
anything at all,
including daring
to remember
all we have been

and daring to
forgive, even
ourselves.

II.
This is a time
when little things
unexpectedly
assume great
consequence:

standing up,
sitting down,
walking to the other
side of the room,
reaching across
the table for
a muffin.

The forward looking
world suddenly seems
a strange place to live
as tenuous memories
now tend to usurp
the primacy of plans
and expectations.

The old demons
still rage but even
they find it
difficult to gain
a foothold in order
to assert a commanding
relevance.

Actually, the question
of relevance
becomes thematic
as does a certain
underlying angst.

It is nothing new,
perhaps even trite
when seen by others,
this final tottering

rite of passage into
the preordained
slippage of the gears,
this falling away
of firm holds,
this kind of

disenfranchisement
from the world.

It is easy to feel
out of place
and remote,
easy to rail
against the state
of things
which seems so
suddenly to have
come to pass,

easy to fear both
the unknown
and the commonplace,

and perhaps too easy
to fear the day
you'll look in the mirror
and see only
a distant relative
of yourself
whose misplaced
name is turning
over and over
on the tip of your
tractionless
and muted
tongue.

Change

All is change,
Heraclitus said.

Standing in a river
we can feel the flow
of ever new water
on its way to
the inconstant sea.

So it may be,

but perhaps time
is not a line
but a loop

and tomorrow
comes round
from yesterday

and today is then and now
and is yet to come.

Perhaps things are
always different,
yet always the same

and human nature
will never change.

Death of a Poem

The poem I wrote today
was nearly perfect,
perhaps the best poem
I have ever written

but I am not one to brag.

Let's just say that,
after rereading
it several times
and making a few tweaks
here and there,
I was satisfied
with its easy cadence
and nuanced meaning.

It reminded me
of a Tibetan sand painting,
intricate and beautiful

and perhaps this is why,
after printing it out
and reading it one last time,

I erased it from the hard drive
and took the only printed page
outside on the deck

and there,
in a soft breeze
beneath a few early stars,
set it on fire

and watched
as the bright flames
briefly raged.

Darkness

It will be a different
kind of darkness.

The darkness
I am talking about
will not come
from a failure
of the power grid,
or from volcanic ash
enveloping the globe,
or from debris
driven into
the stratosphere
by a random
asteroid strike.

It will not come
from a nuclear winter.

The darkness
I am talking about
will be disguised
as light.

It will seem like summer
and blooming flowers
and smiles all around.

It will seem like picnics
and the 4th of July.

It will come upon us
so gradually
we won't even
recognize it

until it's too late.

One Autumn Evening

Clouds shamble
across the sky
like bewildered
refugees from some
nameless horror.

They move north
where they will soon
be dismembered
by upper level winds
or turned into
dancing angels
with tumultuous eyes.

So it goes
with the sky.

I gaze earthward
and see freshly
fallen leaves
thickly covering
the ground,
looking like layers
of exhausted
question marks

while the trees
stand tall,
exulting in their
new found
nakedness.

If I Am Honest With Myself

If I am honest
with myself,
I have to admit
that true self-forgiveness
can be the most grueling
path to peace of mind,
but also the most
necessary.

Even in the absence
of evil intent,
the everyday failures
of a human life
build up
like artery plaque
or coal dust
in the lungs

because there is no cure
for being human.

It is a matter
of accepting
and living with
the clinging burden
of imperfection.

Though scarred
and wounded
by my own missteps,
I have to forgive myself
over and over
so that I can move on,
so that I can meet
each new day
on something like
equal terms.

Streets of the Night

The fickle
and treacherous
streets of the night
go on and on.

They lead to calumny
and infamy
and broken dreams

and they smile
as they plunge off
old bridges
and abandoned
ship piers.

They shrug
as they dead end
in dark places
with no names

and yet they go
on and on
with unsettling
vigor and
echoing laughter

as they become
back roads and
interstates,
byways and turnpikes,

and metaphors
without end.

Dung Beetle and Eye Winkers

It's amazing
what you can learn
before you even
get out of bed
in the morning.

Dung beetles
chart their course
using the Milky Way
while they
push 2,000 times
their own weight
in gazelle shit
over the African
savannah.

Eye winkers
are a very
poetic name
for errant lashes,
that is,
of the optical
type.

There are worse ways
to start the day…

Thinking Back 60 Years, Remembering Sam

It would have
been best
not to look
into his eyes
at the moment
of sudden
realization,
right before
the first shot
rang out.

And best not
to look
as he fell
in an ungraceful
heap after
the second shot
finished him
off.

It would have
been best
not to watch
as they hooked
him and hung him
upside down
from the tripod
and slit
his throat
and his
steamy blood
ran out
into the big
porcelain pot.

It would have
been best
not to smell
the boiling hair
in the cast
iron kettle
or watch

the quick knives
do their work
on the butcher table
or see the dogs
fighting for pieces
of his heart
and lungs.

It would have
been best
just to eat
the sausage
and the bacon
and the ham
biscuits
later on
and not think
about our
former barnyard
buddy to whom
we felt so compelled
to give the name
of Sam.

Looking

I'm looking
for the poems
which have never
made it
to the surface
of light

the ones which lurk
half formed,
inchoate,
in the shadows
at the edge
of my life.

I am looking
for the poems
without names
whose troubled
voices

press me
at odd hours
to bring them forth
so they may
be heard

once and for all
for better or worse.

Jump

Blue flame or white,
acetylene burns hot.

The torch spits its
fiery arc,
but will the weld hold?

Junk yard scrap
can become
a sculpted marvel
or remain a pile of
oxidized dreams
beneath an
unforgiving sun.

It is a risk
some of us
choose to take,
trammeled by time
and crooked chance,
hemmed in
by chain link
fences of
our own making,
scorched by
hope's relentless
blaze,

doing our best
to break free.

On the Porch

Heat lightning
over the bay,
desultory ruminations
on a tottering porch,
a shadow creeps
along the creek bottom.

The past walks
home from the future
over the marsh,
bent and almost
unrecognizable,
its eyes glazed
with forbidden
knowledge.

What auguries are these?

My thoughts are
but vague ambiguities
blurred around the edges
like cedar tumps
in the sea mist.

Must I
Rorschach the clouds?
Read the entrails
of bewildering dreams?
Chart the osprey's
swoops and dives?

I close my eyes
and listen
to the rising wind.

Truth Be Told

Truth be told
we are mostly empty space,
organic formulae
ghostly as neutrinos,
walking the earth
under the illusion
of free will
and our own majesty.

Truth be told
we are incautious
alchemists
teetering
on the verge
of our own extinction

the line between
carbon and silicon
soon to be blurred
beyond recognition,

blurred by ourselves,
the prize seekers,
who will create
our own redundancy,
our own lack
of relevance,
just part of a process
we misunderstand.

No bombs,
no Armageddon,
no bangs,
no whimpers,
just a low hum
or electronic
whisper.

Rancor

Exhausted by
the scrum of life
and feeling
homicidal,
I want to slit
rancor's vile throat
with a well-honed
oyster knife,
let it bleed out
beneath the moon
on the cold ground,
let it rot in place
all the winter long
to fertilize
spring dandelions

or better yet,
drag it down
to the marsh
on a flood tide,
weight it down
with ballast stones,
let its carbuncled
corpse be picked
clean by crabs
in the shallows.

My New Book

My new book of poems
lies on the table.

I think it turned out
decently.
It has a good feel,
an ample but
non-ponderous weight.
The cover is compelling,
even intriguing.
The text is proofed
and edited to
near perfection.
The layout is pleasing.

Yet, already I am tired
of these poems
and I am sure they
are tired of me.

I dream that
they have absconded
en masse,
leaving behind nothing
but blank pages
and the table of contents.

When I wake,
I resolve not
to read the book again
until I can pretend
in earnest that
it was written
by someone else.

Soldiers of Fortune

Forces beyond our ken,
some from without
some from within,

make a mystery
of what we see
and who we are

of what we have been
and what we
will someday be.

Yet we remain
soldiers of fortune
driven by the lust
for power
over ourselves
and our world

and we soldier on.

When we finally storm
the fortresses
and breach
the walled cities
of our own
labyrinthine minds

what will we find?

An inner sanctum
of holy writs
and glimmering gems

or dead end alleyways
and wandering streets
leading nowhere
in particular?

My Days

I am at that age
where I find myself
trying to wring
all the succulence
from each passing
day

but falling short
time and time again.

The marrow
of the days
eludes my grasp,

the sweet juices
of the days
turn to water
and then to air
in my jaws.

Part of me wants
to notch my
remaining days
like a gunslinger,
but to what avail?

It is not quantity
but the quality
that matters.

It is about
the succulence
after all.

Late March 2020

How hard it must be to live only with what one knows and what one remembers, cut off from what one hopes for!
- Albert Camus, *The Plague*

I
Outside my porch windows
a long sunset colors the sky
in vivid orange, red, and gold
and after it fades, Venus appears
unusually bright in the west,
the closest it has been in years.
The somehow eerie simplicity
of this scene makes my heart ache
with a sadness I cannot put
into words.

II
In Wuhan province,
after initial bungling,
the Chinese government
reacted by welding shut
the doors of apartment buildings
to force inhabitants to stay inside.
They have finally emerged,
shaken but alive for now.

In America, our leaders allowed
Florida beaches to remain open,
densely packed with worshippers
of thoughtless fun who then departed,
bringing unwelcome surprises
to their far flung homes.

III
Nothing but impermanence lasts.
Yet I wash my hands thirteen times a day
and fear the eventual lack of ventilators
in my small rural community.
My dreams have claustrophobia
as a recurring theme.
All this, while doctors and nurses
in New York don garbage bags

for protection in ICU suicide wards
as refrigerated trucks wait in the streets
to accept the inevitable overflow
from crowded morgues.

IV
My wife returns from the grocery store
and I put on latex gloves to help her
bring in the bulging plastic bags.

These days, nothing I do dispels
for long my feeling
of helplessness and a vague
sense of uncontrollable grief.
As I unpack the groceries
I find myself wondering
if I even deserve to live,
but we all know deserving
has nothing to do with it.

V
The surreal has become
commonplace
and the commonplace
has become surreal.
I feel like a ghost of myself
who cannot shake hands,
who cannot embrace friends
and loved ones,
who cannot even touch
my own troubled face.

When All Has Been Taken From Me

When all has been
taken from me,
let me lie down
alone beneath
the stars.

When all has been
taken from me,
let me sleep
in silence
beneath the sea.

Do not wake me
to say the merciless
moon is seeking me
beneath the waves,
plaintively,

far into the deep.

About the Author

Kendall Bradley is a native of Accomack County on the Eastern Shore of Virginia and holds B.A. and M.A. degrees from the University of Virginia. Unlike most Shore natives and many of the "come heres," he does not hunt and fish but nonetheless can appreciate the enduring magic of this narrow spit of land felicitously wedged between the Atlantic Ocean and the Chesapeake Bay. Every now and then, he types a few lines on his laptop which sometimes, by a strange alchemy of sorts, are transformed into something that can loosely be termed "poetry." Kendall lives with his lovely wife, muse, and best friend, Ronda, in the small town of Melfa, a community which sprang up when the railroad came through in 1884 and which straddles the now abandoned track and Lankford Highway, a portion of U.S. Route 13 which, it is said, once ran from Maine to Florida and perhaps still does. *At the Edge of Mercy* is his fourth book of poetry. Other books by the author include *Backwater Moon*, *A Butterfly with Teeth*, and *Vicinity of Time*.

www.ingramcontent.com/pod-product-compliance
Lightning Source LLC
Chambersburg PA
CBHW070855050426
42453CB00012B/2212